The Hall Of Fame Game Collection:

Stop Simping And
START PIMPING

How To Get Women By Using Pimping Instead Of Simping

Written By
The Professor Of Pimpology

Famous Words Of A PIMP:

"It's not matrimony, it's macaroni."

-Pimpin Ken

Famous Words Of A SIMP:

"I'm not a simp, I-I just respect women."

-Unknown

© **Copyright 2023 by** The Door 2 Success Publishing - **All rights reserved.**

This document is geared towards providing exact and reliable information in regards to the topic and issue covered.

The publication is sold with the idea that the publisher is not required to render accounting, officially permitted, or otherwise, qualified services. If advice is necessary, legal or professional, a practiced individual in the profession should be ordered.

From a Declaration of Principles which was accepted and approved equally by a Committee of the

American Bar Association and a Committee of Publishers and Associations.

In no way is it legal to reproduce, duplicate, or transmit any part of this document in either electronic means or in printed format. Recording of this publication is strictly prohibited and any storage of this document is not allowed unless with written permission from the publisher. All rights reserved.

The information provided herein is stated to be truthful and consistent, in that any liability, in terms of inattention or otherwise, by any usage or abuse of any policies, processes, or directions contained within is the solitary and utter responsibility of the recipient reader.

Under no circumstances will any legal responsibility or blame be held against the publisher for any reparation, damages, or monetary loss due to the information herein, either directly or indirectly.

Respective authors own all copyrights not held by the publisher. The information herein is offered for informational purposes solely, and is universal as so. The presentation of the information is without contract or any type of guarantee assurance.

The trademarks that are used are without any consent, and the publication of the trademark is without permission or backing by the trademark owner. All trademarks and brands within this book are for clarifying purposes only and are then owned by the owners themselves, not affiliated with this document.

Don't Simp, Pimp

"You're always applying Pimp Principles, or Simp Principles."

A pimps always puts money over women, while a simp puts women over everything. That's why he'll pay his way just to be around women. Simps are the major clients of a pimp, strip clubs and porn sites.

Businesses preying on a simps money creates billion dollar industries that are run by pimps. That pimp understood that if he sold the product of women that he'll never be without money. All because a simp will pay his money for her honey.

A pimp views women as someone who can make him money instead of personal pussy or a wife. To a pimp a woman's value is what she can do to get him more money for his pockets.

A pimp keeps his mind on "How can she get me more money?", not how can I get access to her honey. He keeps his eyes on the real prize, instead of what's between her thighs.

He understands that pussy feels good for a moment, but having money makes me feel good for a lifetime. This is the long term thinking that a simp disregards for his instant gratification of short term pleasure.

The simp doesn't understand that no pussy is going to feel better than the satisfaction of his hard work coming to fruition. Making a woman the center of his world just for the motivation of having pussy around will always be his downfall.

As a man you spend more time listening to her mouth than banging her pussy anyway. So what's better than having access to her honey and getting her to pay you instead?

A pimp leads a woman with his mouthpiece and not his wallet like the simp or the trick. Because if you lead her with your mouthpiece she will always respect your mouthpiece. If you lead her with money she will always only respect your money.

So if your money runs dry she'll just leave you for another man who can fill her pockets like you used to. You want a woman to respect your mouthpiece because that comes to you for free and it will last forever as long as you keep your game tight.

The trick is called a trick because he's too lazy to put the work into her mind himself. He just decides to shortcut the whole process and pay the game with his hard earned money for her pussy. But he never gets the woman or her respect in the process.

While the simp spends his valuable time acting like he wants to "get to know her" for the pussy. She uses him while he wastes his money and his irreplaceable time, both he will never get back.

The simp always gets a bad deal and gets tricked by the woman in the process because he'll never get his money's worth from just getting the pussy. He loses her respect in the long run because he views the woman as a prize and not himself.

All because her pussy is the prize he's after, he will compromise his values, his self esteem, his time and energy just for 20 minutes of pussy. Not realizing that her pussy is free to her, but his money takes time from his life for him to earn.

The simp's elevation of her pussy won't even allow him to stand up to a woman and say how he really feels, just because he's fearful she will take access to her pussy away from him.

Ultimately the simp loses his self respect and the pimp keeps her self respect. Because the pimp doesn't elevate the woman over himself he can look in the mirror with confidence that he hasn't compromised his value to a woman just for pussy.

If You Enjoy Learning About The Game:

@theprofessorofpimpology

All Wisdom Works If You Work It!

The Definition Of Simpology

Simpology refers to the psychological study behind why a man puts himself in a non masculine position of submission under a woman just to fulfill his desire for pussy.

Simpology and the study of its psychology looks at why a man lets a woman abuse and manipulate his emotions to gain the position of superiority and dominance in any type of relationship.

The only psychology principles that can change a Simpology mindset of a man into a psychology of dominance and masculinity are the principles of Pimpology.

Once a man learns the concepts of Pimpology he abandons his simpology belief system and then becomes the type of man that women of all races, cultures and belief systems desire to mate with.

The Definition Of Pimpology

Pimpology refers to the study of Pimping and the psychology behind it. Pimpology teaches principles that show you how to control and manipulate others, by understanding the principles of human psychology.

Pimpology is effective because most people have no knowledge of brain psychology. This makes their minds extremely vulnerable to those who understand the basic principles. Pimpology is the study of these basic principles.

These principles make up the techniques and mindsets learned in this wisdom. And these principles named Pimpology empower an individual to manipulate the minds of others and move them into action.

This is what Pimpology is and what Pimpology does for the individual who becomes a Master. The one who studies Pimpology will be rewarded greatly with the knowledge of self and others. Therefore also learning the unconscious habits of the human mind.

"Nice Guy", Learn From The PIMP Game

Nice guys, you are the most manipulative and dishonest type of guy that exists in the kingdom of men. You say the opposite of how you really feel or even worse for you, you say nothing and just hold it inside.

Why are you this fake character in life, in bondage to your need to please and be liked? You're a people pleaser and self sacrificer who has a hard time being disliked. Fuck that! Those days are over if you want to do any kind of pimping.

If you don't like yourself, it doesn't mean shit if anyone and everyone else in the world likes you. Odds are they won't like being around your needy ass anyway. In this game confidence is everything! You hear me?

Your problem is:

• You're afraid of conflict so you back down because you "Don't like to fight"

• You need others to "Like you"

• You need everyone to approve of your dreams and ideas

- You always have friends around you "You don't like to be alone"

- You let girls say whatever they feel, but you avoid speaking your mind because "You don't like to fight"

- You let women set the rules and you let her control the direction of the relationship

- You do things you don't want to instead of saying no, then complain in your head about it

- Everything you do and think about centers around getting women or having sex

You don't understand who you are as a man. So instead of saying how you feel when you feel it you hold onto it and make an excuse for yourself to be okay with it. Stop! You let the nice guy "Character" lead your life instead of manhood leading your life.

So you need women, your family, your friends and everyone else to validate you as a "Nice man" instead of a "Powerful man". And you know what most women do to "nice guys" right? Look at your past experiences, did she not use you and abuse you?

Did she then not find her way out the door with the next guy she was talking to, while with you on social media or dating apps? See "Nice guy" All she has to do is stroke your ego, remove your defenses and take advantage of your weakness to sex.

Just as a black widow uses seduction to weaken its prey and as Delilah seduced Samson for her gain. Ultimately only leading to the loss of freedom and life for the man who fell into the hypnotic rhythm of her seduction trap.

When you act super nice and friendly all the time, women can sense this "nice guy" vulnerability in you. She can see and feel how insecure and uncomfortable you become, when powerful and confident men are around.

Women are so intuitive she can feel your energy shift. You can have a lot of women as the "nice guy" but let me be the one to be honest with you, they're all using you for your benefits.

If you're okay with trading your time, attention, money and sex for free just for pussy, you're a trick. That's the other side of the game, so pimping ain't for you. Just keep on tricking, thank you, you keep the game alive.

Nice guys attract masculine girls because opposites attract. You attract a masculine woman because you're a feminine man. Your soft and feminine

"Nice guy" energy pushes your woman to feel more masculine around you.

In any two people there is always one submitting and one leading. When both people try to lead fights are created. As a nice guy you try to overcompensate.

Your only game is to use your money, your muscles, your car but never your game alone to attract a woman. Your need to be seen and to show what you have shows your hidden insecurity and your lack of confidence in your game.

Nice guys believe in love over respect. So you think that love feelings alone will keep her with you but you're wrong because her love is much less important to her than her respect.

A Pimp understands that she must respect you more than she loves you at all times. If she loves you but doesn't respect you, it's only a matter of time before she'll leave you because "love" is a fading feeling.

But if she loves you but she respects you more, her respect can last forever even after the love fades away as long as you stay a respectable man. Respect weighs more than love!

Nice guy, you believe in a fairytale love like a woman. Love is a superficial feeling based upon how you act, so you can't rely on love because someones love can change at any moment.

You can't build your life in any way with anyone on a feeling that can change in a second. You're willing to play the sideline or on her backup bench with all of the other simps she collects in her phone and on her social media.

You'll sit around and wait for her to choose you instead of dealing with women who choose you. That's simp behavior! Women only use and manipulate the "nice guy" for emotional attention.

She never intends to keep you. But to keep you around she sells you dreams just as a pimp would do his hoes. Flip the game around and move as she moves.

There are plenty of "Nice girls" out here on the sidelines waiting to pay to play with a man because they're lonely and desperate. Take pussy off the table when you talk to her and put money on the table instead and watch how her game falls apart.

As a man in a world of women you need to meet a new woman and immediately think, How can she advance my future? What skills does this woman have that benefits my future?

Because this is exactly all she's thinking about when she meets you and starts her interview process. She wants your sex eventually or else she wouldn't have chosen you out of other men in the first place.

There had to be some sexual attraction in her choice of you. Once you understand how women play the game then you're equipped to play the game with knowledge.

Then once you learn the mentality you need to play the game, you're now equipped to play the game with wisdom and skill. See women have one game, and one game they play only. Women can only play the game cat and mouse.

Her pussy is the cat and your scary ass is the frightened little mouse, running around afraid of what you really want to say and feel. Believe me, she laughs with her friends about how she controls your emotions and your happiness.

Then when the fun is over, she kills your emotions by cheating with your best friend or by sleeping with someone you both knew together. This is the fate of the "nice guy".

"Stop being the mouse and become the cat and make her play her role, she wants to."

Table Of Pimping

Don't Simp, Pimp	8
The Definition Of Simpology	15
The Definition Of Pimpology	17
"Nice Guy", Learn From The PIMP Game	19

The SIMP Mindset   **36**

Dear Simp,	37
The Most Famous Simp Of ALL Time	47
The Symptoms Of Simping (SOS)	53
What Creates A Simp?	56

SIMP To PIMP Reprogramming   **64**

A Pimp Vs A Simp	66
Never Submit Your Power To Beauty	70
Never Choose Anyone Over Your Dreams	75
Purpose First, Pussy Second	79
Pussy Isn't Payment For Your Value	86

Stop Thinking Like A Trick	94
Always Be Better Than Her	98
Never Do These Things With A Woman	104
Dress to Impress	112
You're Not Her Fan, You're Her Man	116
She's In Love With "Love" Not You	125
Her Respect Weighs More Than Her Love	145
Seduce Her Mind And Her Body Follows	152
Exactly How To Seduce Her Mind	159
Listen And Learn Her Desires	168
Lead Her With Words, Not Money	179
Real Game Separates You From The Lames	185
How To Give Her Game	188
Lying Isn't Real Game, It's Lame	198
Why The Lying Game Doesn't Work	202
Simps Lack Real Game	206

Learn How To Play "Hide The Dick" 212

Make Her Invest Her Time & Money In You 218

You Don't Own Her, You Just Loan Her 225

There's No Loyalty In This Game 229

3 PIMP Pick up Techniques 232

Courting Technique: How To Get A Woman Obsessed 234

Club/Bar Pickup Technique: The "Fly Fishing" Strategy 241

Manipulation Technique: Reversing The Game On A Gold Digger 246

Simp Heres The Truth…

"She doesn't want "you" as a person, she only wants what "you" can DO for her! Just stop doing for her and then you'll see."

THE SIMP MINDSET

Dear Simp,

Simp,

You are the most manipulative and dishonest type of guy that exists in the kingdom of men. Why? Because you say the opposite of how you really feel or even worse for you, you say nothing and just hold it inside.

Why are you this fake character in life, in bondage to your need to please and be liked? You're a people pleaser and self sacrificer who has a hard time being disliked. Fuck that! Those days are over if you want to do any kind of pimping.

If you don't like yourself, it doesn't mean shit if anyone else in the world likes you. Odds are they won't like being around your needy ass anyway. In this game confidence is everything! You hear me?

Your problem is:

• You're afraid of conflict so you back down because you "Don't like to fight"

• You need others to "Like you"

• You need everyone to approve of your dreams and ideas

- You always have friends around you "You don't like to be alone"

- You let girls say whatever they feel, but you avoid speaking your mind because "You don't like to fight"

- You let women set the rules and you let her control the direction of the relationship

- You do things you don't want to instead of saying no, then complain in your head about it

- Everything you do and think about centers around getting women or having sex

You don't understand who you are as a man. So instead of saying how you feel when you feel it you hold onto it and make an excuse for yourself to be okay with it. Stop!

You let the nice guy "Character" lead your life instead of your manhood leading your life. So you need women, your family, your friends and everyone else to validate you as a "Nice man" instead of a "Powerful man".

And you know what most women do to "nice guys" right? Look at your past experiences, did she not use you and abuse you? Did she not cheat with your friends, men at her work or men she met at bars and clubs?

Did she then not find her way out the door with the next guy she was talking to on social media or dating apps? See "Nice guy" All she has to do is stroke your ego, remove your defenses and take advantage of your weakness to sex.

Just as a black widow uses seduction to weaken its prey and as Delilah seduced Samson for her gain. Ultimately only leading to the loss of freedom and life for the man who fell into the hypnotic rhythm of her seduction trap.

When you act super nice and friendly all the time, women can sense this "nice guy" vulnerability in you. She can see and feel how insecure and uncomfortable you become when powerful and confident men are around.

Women are so intuitive they can feel when your energy shifts. You can have a lot of women as the "nice guy simp" but let me be the one to be honest with you, they're all using you for your benefits.

If you're okay with trading your time, attention, money and sex for free just for pussy, you're a trick. You believe in a fairytale love just like a woman does.

But her "love" is a superficial feeling based upon how you act, so you can't rely on love because someones love can change at any moment. And you can't build your life in any way with anyone based upon a feeling that can change in a second.

She has to respect you much more than she "loves" you and how can she respect you if you submit to her every need and want? When she respects you she won't do you wrong even if she leaves you out of her respect for you.

She will always have a place in her heart for a man she respects but she will always have a place in her pocket to use the man she "loves". As a man in a world of women you must meet a new woman and immediately think:

1. How can she advance my future?

2. What skills does this woman have that benefits my future?

Because this is exactly all she's thinking about when she meets you and starts her interview process. She wants sex eventually or she wouldn't have chosen you out of the other men in the first place. But her focus is on what can you do for her.

Once you understand how women play the game then you're equipped to play the game with knowledge and strategy. Once you learn mentally how to play the game, you're now equipped to play the game of women with wisdom and skill.

Women have only one game, and one game they play only. Women can only play the game of cat and mouse. Her pussy is the cat and your fear to be yourself is the frightened little mouse, afraid to say what you really want to say and feel.

As she laughs with her friends about how she controls your emotions and your happiness. Then when the fun is over, she kills your emotions by cheating with your best friend or by sleeping with someone you both knew together.

This is the fate of the simp. Stop being the mouse and become the cat and make her play her role of the mouse like she wants to. If you act like other men you get what other men get. There's a reason a pimp gets what he wants and a simp gets played.

The Most Famous Simp Of ALL Time

*Based Upon The Story Of Samson & Delilah

Samson in his time was known as the "The Warrior & The Judge". He was the ultimate Alpha in looks because he had the strength of a man who was feared and the power of reputation or what we would call fame today.

So he had the external qualities of a desired man, but he had the internal qualities of a Simp. These qualities were his uncontrolled and Un channelled lust for women and his inability to understand that a woman easily manipulates a pussy minded man.

Samson had the gifts of God that are still given to all men today which are the ability to lead, build and create. But he allowed himself to be distracted and easily lured away from his life mission and purpose because of his desire for pussy.

And because he allowed the allure of pussy to take him away from his focus and his mission as a man, he fell into the chaos and destruction that only a lost woman can bring a man who's built to lead but follows pussy instead.

Samson inevitably fell into a life of captivity, sorrow and destruction because he chose women over his purpose. Too much focus on women and your desire for pussy will take you off of your purpose and lead you into a life of chaos just like Samson.

Men are visual by nature so they're naturally attracted by what entices their eyes. This is why women have the shape that they do, they are built to attract you. So her looks and her body is her edge in the mating and dating game against you.

So if you allow your attraction to a woman's beauty or your desire for her booty to pull you away from the internal mission that you have in life, you'll always find yourself manipulated by the emotional intelligence of a woman.

That's because while a man chases his desire for sex and female interaction, a woman uses her attraction to subtract the resources that a man works hard to attain in life. There are many examples of modern day Samson's.

- Strong & Attractive Men
- Wealthy Men
- Athletes
- Entertainers

You hear stories all the time about these men who worked hard to attain status above other men, only to have what they've worked so hard to earn taken away by a woman who used her attraction to get access to sometimes half of a man's resources.

Just like Samson was heavily led by what he saw in a woman's external appearance these men are also. It's because they get so focused on a woman's external appearance that they ignore the many red flags in their mind saying "danger".

Don't be like Samson because he lost in the game of women. Let him be an example to you of how even the strongest of men are taken down by the manipulative prowess of a cunning woman.

Money, fame, status and a man's looks don't keep him from being a simp like Samson. It's your mentality and the ability to transcend your desires to look deeper into a woman's energy that gives you your edge when you're dealing with women.

You don't just get a woman's body, you get her mind. Her beauty fades over time but her mind can benefit you as you strive to become the most successful version of yourself in life if used right.

So either you'll Simp like Samson and find yourself at the mercy of a woman's mental and physical manipulation or you'll Pimp and put her at the mercy of your mental strategy! You Decide!

The Symptoms Of Simping (SOS)

• Going overboard to impress a female that doesn't like you

• Saying thirsty things like 'Where's my hug at?' Or "Can I get a kiss?"

• You're always looking for a woman or girlfriend because you're "lonely"

• You put women and their attention above yourself and your self esteem

• You're easy to defend feminist beliefs

- You're uncomfortable with any negative talk about women

- You use money, cars and fancy clothes solely to win a woman's approval

- You always do what she asks but she never does what you ask

- You allow women to determine your self esteem

- The woman has all of the say in your relationships and you have little to none

- You stay on the phone all day and night with her

- You dedicate your whole thought life to her

- She rants to you about her relationship problems and you listen, but she gets disinterested when you talk

- She takes hours to call and respond to your messages, but you respond immediately

- You put women over money and you lead with your wallet

- You can't tell a woman 'NO"

What Creates A Simp?

Reason #1: He has a lack of female attention and acceptance presently in life and or growing up. He may have lacked female validation in their younger years so they seek it out desperately as they get older to fulfill their desire for women.

Maybe as teens and or as grown men he was considered to be ugly and unattractive by the women that he desire the most. He could've been teased or rejected by important women like his mother or girls he had crushes on in school.

Reason #2: He has negative and belittling parents or siblings. This is why a healthy family structure is necessary for a man to have when growing up. Abusive parents create needy, emotionally weak and angry children who become simps.

Likely he had a negative and abusive mother, father or siblings that took the opportunities to destroy his self esteem instead of build it up. Bullying siblings like mean big sisters cause a simp to desperately desire being accepted by girls.

Reason #3: He feels worthless and low value inside himself. A man with a low self esteem will always look to be a people pleaser because he wants someone to want and accept him. He will sacrifice his self esteem just to gain approval of women.

He can have the best parents and family structure but if he has very low confidence and a negative self perception of his value he will be his own worst enemy. So he needs the validation of a woman to make him feel like he's valuable.

Reason #4: He had a past bad breakup that hurt and traumatized him. Now the pain of rejection and hurt from a past breakup pushes him to project all of his needy energy onto his future relationships.

So now he tries even harder not to lose the next woman so he gets needy and clingy which ultimately pushes the woman away anyway. He needs a woman in his life to feel complete because of the pain of his relationship trauma.

Reason #5: He's in love with the idea of a fairy tale love, just like a woman was taught to believe in as a child. So he believes that his soul mate will one day find him and everything will be perfect just like in the movies.

The thought of being in love drives his lonely and needy behaviors of finding "the one" because he bought in mentally to all of the Disney movies messages of a fairy tale love and marriage as a little boy.

Reason #6: He believes the messages taught by feminism. Men are told they're displaying toxic masculinity if they speak up for themselves or talk about what characteristics they want in a woman.

And because powerful manhood qualities are rarely represented in the media, real masculinity looks negative to him. So he's bought into the idea of the happy wife, happy life motto.

Reason #7: He knows that it's safe to be a simp. It's a guarantee that he will get girls if he acts as a submissive man. But the problem is a submissive man only attracts masculine women.

He doesn't have to fight with his woman because she's always right even if he doesn't agree with her. So his relationships have less conflict but in turn he's compromising himself and his self confidence in the process.

Reason #8: He was raised by a single mother. As a child of a single mother a boy is taught how to be submissive and subservient to a woman under the label of her teaching him how to become a "good man".

A mother teaches her son how to be the perfect man for her so he learns as a child how to be led by the demands of a woman to get along. A woman can't teach a man how to be a logical man, she can only teach him how to be an emotional man.

Reason #9: He likes the comfort of being the "nice guy" personality. It's comfortable and doesn't ruffle feathers when you stay safe as the 'Nice Guy". But the problem is people like you, but don't respect you.

This makes a relationship for a simp very difficult because a woman's respect weighs more than her love. Respect stays while emotions sway back and forth depending on the day. The nice guy wins friends but always loses himself in the end.

SIMP TO PIMP REPROGRAMMING

"Never be mentally and physically married to a woman who didn't say "I do" to you."

-The Professor Of Pimpology

A Pimp Vs A Simp

There are 2 types of men:

1. Pimps

2. Simps

Every man is either a pimp or a simp

a. Pimps are masculine men

b. Simps are feminized men

Whichever energy governs you, will determine if you're a pimp or a simp. The masculine man has a feminine side, but his masculine side is where he is the most comfortable.

A woman prefers a simp to take care of the house and the kids because he's submissive and doesn't fight when she tells him what to do. She can treat the simp with disrespect because she knows he won't go anywhere because she has the power.

She prefers the pimp sexually and sees him as strong, attractive energetically and masculine. She wants the pimp to own her body and take control of the power because she is really submissive in her nature. She desires a man who takes charge.

She trusts the pimp with her body but she trusts the simp to take care of her needs because he has pedestalized her over himself and his own needs. The reason why simps cheat is because they never tell their woman how they "really" feel.

This over time makes him resentful and he takes that out on a woman by being passive aggressive and sneaky. Simps traumatize most women because they're afraid of saying what they mean because of the fear of losing the woman.

Simps hold their feelings in, say things to not get her angry and they give her the position of power which is a burden for a woman in the relationship.

They've submitted their masculine power and traded their dignity for the pursuit of pussy.

Never Submit Your Power To Beauty

Focusing on the woman's beauty alone is a formula for disaster. That's because you'll accept all kinds of red flag behaviors from her that you wouldn't normally accept due to your lust and desire to get her in bed.

When you elevate your desire for sex over your desire to understand her mind you're already at a disadvantage and she's at an advantage. When you lust for her body and pay very little attention to her mindset now she's in the position of power.

It's no different than when a woman likes you because of your looks, money, status etc. you're in the position of power because she's not paying attention to your mindset. This is why it's dangerous to put a woman's body over her mind.

Not only will you look past red flags, your lust for her body will push you to see her in your eyes as the prize in the relationship. And when a woman feels like she's the prize in your life her respect levels for you will always diminish over time.

When a woman knows that she's the prize she feels powerful because she now has the ability to take advantage of you in every way possible. This is how a woman gains access to the money, power and resources of wealthy and famous men everyday.

These men have elevated her body and her beauty as the prize, but they never took enough time to really understand her mind and her motives until it's too late. When they finally see who she is on the inside she's already gotten his resources.

You have to be smarter than these men and deal with beautiful women from a position of power to guard yourself from being taken advantage of. This means you must get to know her mind and her motivations instead of being infatuated by lust.

Her beauty and her booty may get her in the gate but her mind will either keep her there or get her thrown out. Beautiful women are the most deceptive in the game because beauty has power.

External beauty is intoxicating because it has a magical effect on men. For example, when a man sees a beautiful woman they assume that she's smart and trustworthy because of her beauty. This is called the halo effect in psychology.

<u>The Pimp Mindset</u>: That's why beautiful women are often the most dangerous in the game of dating and relationships. Regardless of how beautiful she

is on the outside, treat her like her beauty doesn't matter despite how much you lust for her.

Regardless of how beautiful her face is, or how banging her body is, if there is nothing inside her mind then you're wasting your time. Just because she's pretty doesn't mean that she's valuable. Because beauty without character means nothing!

You can't work with a woman who's beautiful on the outside but hideous on the inside. She'll always bring you misery. Regardless of how beautiful her parts may be, if she doesn't bring you peace, open the door and lead her back to the streets.

Never Choose Anyone Over Your Dreams

If you choose a romantic relationship over your dreams you will always live with the regret of an unfulfilled desire. So make it clear when you meet someone who wants to be a part of your life that your dream will be number 1.

Tell a woman before you enter into a relationship with her that you'll do anything for her except give up on your dreams and your goals in life. Because if you have to be less than what you desire in life to be just to be with her, you can't be with her.

You'll give her:

-Monogamy

-Loyalty

-Money

You can't give up on your dreams, goals and desires in life for anything or anyone, even yourself. If you have to give up on an idea that drives your life and surrender the pursuit of your dreams to be with someone, pick being alone every time.

Because if you can abandon your own personal dreams you'll abandon anyone. Your dreams have to be the number one commitment in your life over everything.

Too many people are in extremely unhappy relationships because they gave up on their dream to be with a man or a woman in a relationship. Now they live with the regret of an unrealized dream.

So never let anyone or anything tell you that your dream isn't worth it. Regardless of how possible they see you reaching your dream, believe in yourself because it's the only way it will happen.

If you ever find yourself in a relationship with a woman who questions your ideas, discourages your goals and doesn't add to the mission in your life, she's a distraction.

Any woman who wants to have the privilege of you in her life has to see herself living with you in your dream. If she can't see herself living in your dream with you then she'll always try to discourage you from making it happen.

You never want to be the angry and discouraged man who lives with the regret of an unfulfilled dream and a discouraging woman that kills your dreams. If she can't light the fire of your desire for your goals she has to go!

Purpose First, Pussy Second

As a man on a mission to think and live on a higher level than most men, you must have a very firm understanding that your life purpose is not to have sex with as many women as possible.

This is not the thinking of a focused, purpose led and determined man, this is the thought process of a hormone filled teenage boy. Only lonely and bored men and women have no other purpose than the instant gratification of sex.

This is why the strip clubs, porn sites and social media are so popular and profitable today. These industries prey on the men and the women who don't have the ability to delay gratification of a future accomplished mission and purpose.

By having a clear direction in your head daily, you won't have the time to waste your money or your precious energy on promiscuous and lost women who will only delay the progress of your future achievement.

If your direction in life is solid it's much more difficult for you to fall into the trap of sleeping with lonely and bored women with no direction in life other than a job.

As you're on your mission and striving to create a better and brighter future for yourself, you'll meet women who are doing the same. These are the only women who are worthy of your time.

A focused man in a relationship with an unfocused woman is a formula for disaster. But a relationship with a focused man and a focused woman is a formula for even greater success because they're both focused on a goal greater than themselves.

An idle mind is the devils playground and puts you in the position to make mistakes due to boredom. Too much spare time on your hands puts you at risk of dealing with promiscuous women who will trap you into toxic relationships and pregnancy.

Why do you see so many unhappy men dealing with unhappy and toxic baby mothers? Because during the unfocused times in their lives they automatically focused on the instant gratification and pleasure of chasing pussy.

Because when a man has too much time on his hands, most men will go directly into chasing women. Just listen to the conversations of your friends. How often does the conversation go directly into the topic of women?

Being on your purpose kills your relationship desperation and focuses your attention on things that have meaning in a mans life. Because at the end of your life you'll be more proud of your accomplishments than sexual partner numbers.

Keep goals in your life everyday and keep moving towards your mission. This is what keeps away boredom, depression, hopelessness, loneliness and anxieties about your future.

Your purpose is what keeps you from falling into the trap of settling with a woman below your standards. Because boredom and a lack of purpose in your life will cause you to hold onto toxic relationships longer than you should.

Women are never supposed to be the reason you ever do something, your mission is what leads a man's life. Women and relationships are an add on, and not the motivation for a man who really wants to find greatness in his life.

Experiencing the life you want must be the priority, not experiencing the most pussy like the average man. If a man only lives for sex then he's living at the level of a dog in heat and not a high level thinking man with a desire for greatness.

Be a man on his purpose first before you add a woman into your life. Because you'll always end up much happier and more satisfied with your life in the long run by making your dreams come true.

Pussy Isn't Payment For Your Value

The reason why simps lose with women is they value what she doesn't value. They value what she has between her legs that she gives away for free over their true value as a man which is their time, their attention and their money.

These are the things she values. She values what you have more than she values what she has. That's why women all over the world sell sex for money and trade sex for a mans time and attention commitment.

So if you value something that came for free to her like pussy over what she can offer you which is her mind, her time and her efforts to make your life easier then she'll always get your value and give you in return what she doesn't value. She wins!

She has to first give you something of value, before she can access your value. It's the only way to deal with a woman if you're ready to think like a pimp and not a simp.

She'll never value you if you let her get over on you. Because if she can trade you pussy for your money, your time and your attention you're now in the position of a trick. And a ho will never respect a trick because he got tricked.

He got tricked into valuing what that has no value to her. He got tricked into trading actual value for something of no value, that's the pimp game in a nutshell.

A gold digger uses the same game on a lame to get his money. It doesn't matter if you're rich and you have a lot of money, it's still tricking even if you have it to spend. Because you're still paying value for what she doesn't value.

So you have to flip the game on her head by making her work for your value instead. Show her that her pussy has no value because sex is an even exchange. Sex is a mutually beneficial act unless you act as if her pussy is more important.

Refuse from this point on to ever give up your value to anyone for free and without a fee. Pussy for dick is an even exchange and if you let her think that you having sex with her is an honor and a privilege, she'll charge you time and money for it.

If you don't demand for a woman to give you something more valuable than pussy for payment of your time, money and attention she won't. She'll get you thinking that her pussy is sufficient payment for your resources but it's not.

Any woman you deal with has to offer you her mind and her body, not just her body. But her mind has to always come first because her body will follow automatically if you understand how to use it correctly.

This means that she should be using her mind to make your life easier in some sort of way. The role of a woman in a mans life is to add to the quality of his life. Pussy only adds as a momentary pleasure but it doesn't add to the value of a man.

For example, she should be helping you build your business, paying for her expenses and some of yours, adding to the quality of your lifestyle and she should be using her feminine energy to support the hard work that you do as a man.

Pussy is only the benefit of having you around just like dick is the benefit of her having you around. Pussy has a time and a place but her mind positively and negatively has an impact on every moment of your life.

<u>The Pimp Mindset</u>: Never value her sex over your value which is your protection, your attention and

your resources because that's what separates you from a simp and a pimp.

If you place her sex over your value, she will never respect you as a man because you are easily weakened because of your lust for pussy just like Samson. The weakness of a man is his lust for a woman and women understand this clearly.

A pimp has his options of women because he can't be weaned by his lust for sex. You have to play the game like a pimp plays the game by thinking like the ho instead of the trick.

The trick is a simp because he values pussy over his time and his money. But the pimp is the ho because he makes the woman trade her value to him. Treat your dick, your time and money like the prize and you'll flip the game on her head.

Stop Thinking Like A Trick

A woman doesn't want to be your whole world. Because most women can't handle the pressure of being put on a high pedestal, she knows that she'll inevitably fall from. By nature women are insecure and have a low self esteem.

If you set too high of a standard for her self esteem you'll create the pressure for her to be perfect that she understands she can't live up to. So she'll eventually rebel against the need to be perfect to a lesser man who she can pedestalize.

She wants "you" to have the pressure of being perfect, not her. If she has to be perfect all the time, she can't be freaky sexually like she wants to be out of her fear of looking lesser in your eyes.

She can't handle always acting like a good girl because she isn't regardless of what she looks like. Internally she knows she's putting up a front of being a "good girl", but mentally she thinks the same nasty thoughts as men.

And she'll express these thoughts with the man who lets her be imperfect and feel free to be freaky sexually. The only pedestal she wants to be on, is the pedestal over the other women in your life.

She wants to be the number #1 woman in your life to increase her feeling of security. Because her ego and self esteem is tied into her feeling like she's irreplaceable like Beyonce said in your life.

She wants to be put on the pedestal as the star around other men but she wants you to be the star around other women. She wants other women to envy that she has you and she wants to feel like other men want and desire her.

This social pedestal is the only pedestal you can put her on. The higher you are on the social scale the more important she feels having you next to her.

A woman wants a man who is like a shiny trophy that she can show off to other women and be proud of having. By nature a woman wants a man she can respect and look up to.

Always Be Better Than Her

Women see a man and see marriage, while men see a woman and see sex. This is why so many men eventually end up in toxic and miserable relationships.

They're too focused on who she is on the outside, but not enough on who she is on the inside. If you only see the temporary her, you already see her at a disadvantage while at the same time giving her the advantage.

Why? Because you're looking at her physical body while she's looking at you as a full package. She's looking at your mind and its ability to provide stability for her monetarily, while you're looking at what her body can provide for you sexually.

Now you're at the level of a trick because you're ultimately giving her access to your money for her sex. The only difference is instead of her getting money for sex in one night, she's milking your resources like a cow for a longer amount of time.

But can you blame her? No, you have to blame yourself for playing the game all wrong and for the wrong goals. Sex can never be your only goal for a woman. Sex is the minor goal because eventually in a relationship the sex will get old.

How she can add to your life and how you can use her mind to increase the quality of your life has to always be the greater goal. So make sure her rhythm matches your rhythm.

You can't be with a lazy woman if you're not a lazy man, and you can't have a selfish woman if you're a selfless man. If you're a selfless man, you need a selfless woman. Your energies must match and compliment each other for it to work.

But when it comes to intelligence you have to be smarter than her if you want her trust to let you lead. Your energies must match but your intelligence can't match.

Because a woman won't listen to a man that she thinks she's smarter than. She'll always second guess him. If she starts thinking that she's smarter than you, she'll respect men smarter than her more than you.

This is like leaving the gate open so she can find other higher quality guys. You better be a higher quality man than she is a woman. A woman keeps her respect for a man that she looks up to.

This is why most women often gravitate towards older men. Because they see most men their ages as their peers. And it's harder to be respectful of a mans knowledge that's the same as hers.

<u>The Pimp Mindset</u>: Your job as a man is to always stay intellectually and emotionally smarter than her. This means that you can't stop learning and increasing your knowledge of the world and your woman.

She has to feel like you don't need her for anything and she'll feel like she needs you. If she feels like you can lead her because you're smarter than her, you'll create loyalty.

Love + respect equals a loyal woman. But if she stops respecting you because she's smarter than you she'll leave you and won't mind doing you dirty.

Always be better than her and you'll keep the power and control in the relationship so she'll look to you for your leadership. You should always be bettering yourself, mentally, physically and financially regardless if a woman's in your life or not.

Never Do These Things With A Woman

Never #1: Never lay in bed gossiping about other people, especially other men. Don't be a chatty patty by pillow talking about other peoples lives and other peoples problems, because it'll only make you look weak.

If you gossip about your friends and your families lives then she knows that you'll tell her business also just like she tells other people your business. Women talk to other women a lot so it's hard for them to know something and not tell somebody.

But this is what women do. Women are much more social than men. Let her gossip with her friends and when she starts talking about the lives of others just listen so you know the dirt. Agree but don't engage in the conversation by gossiping also.

Never #2: Never tell her all of your business because she will use it against you if she has to. You must remain a mystery in some ways of your life by keeping your deep secrets and your truly personal business to yourself.

Remember that no woman is guaranteed to stay in your life forever. So if she leaves you then she also leaves with your reputation because she can use all of your deepest secrets that you've told her to make you look bad in the eyes of others.

All it takes is for her to get angry at you and she has all of the personal information that she needs to ruin you or make you extremely upset. This is like giving a woman the ammunition to hurt you, but hoping that she'll never use it. Of course she will!

Never #3: Don't talk about how much money you make or what you have, especially when you first meet a woman. Anytime somebody tries to sell you on their value it lets you know that they see you as higher value than them.

Nobody is attracted to someone who's trying to sell themselves to them, especially a woman. Even if she's attracted to you it won't be for the right reasons. She'll be attracted to your money and what you try to sell her more than you as a person.

Most guys she meets are trying to impress her by selling themselves and their value by talking about or showing off what they have. Don't ever get stuck in the mindset of trying to impress a woman, she should always be selling herself to you instead.

Never #4: Don't talk about how many women that you're sleeping with or have slept with in the past.

This is a big turnoff to her and it makes you look like you're bragging if it's a lot or you have no value if it's very little.

She should always be wondering and assuming so that she never knows exactly how many women you've had in the past. This works to your advantage because she doesn't know exactly which keeps your sense of mystery.

Let her get jealous and wonder if it's a girl you slept with when you see a woman you know when you're both out. If she doesn't think women like you sexually then she won't eventually either.

Never #5: Never talk about other men that you're upset with or jealous of with your woman. That's because it actually has an opposite effect whenever you talk about another man with a woman.

Most men think that they're making the other man look bad by telling his business, but in actuality it makes her more curious about the other man, especially if he's attractive or has a lot of women.

Women see weakness in a man that gossips about other men. When you gossip about another man it makes you look weak and inferior to the other man because he has the power to be on your mind when he's not around.

She'll eventually be looking to find out if the rumors you're telling her are true on her own or she'll use him to get back at you if she's mad at you or you break up. That's because she knows that you already have feelings of dislike for him.

Never #6: Never make a woman you're everything in your life and tell her that she's all you have. If you put all of your eggs in one basket all it takes is for the basket to break and you'll lose everything.

This is why you should never put all of your faith, all of your love and all of your feelings into one woman. No woman can handle the pressure of being a mans everything because it's unfair for her to be more important in your life than you.

You should be your own everything and she should just add to your life. She's not your life and she's not all that you have in life, you are. By giving her too much power to kill your confidence and your joy she will get power hungry and abuse it!

Dress to Impress

You can't say you have game and you don't dress the part. That's because our body language is just as important as the language we speak out of our mouths.

And it's your body language that includes how you dress that attracts a woman's attention or repels it. If you don't dress well and present your best self wherever you go, then women won't see you.

You want a woman to see you and be in awe of you and what you represent on the outside so you can show her who you are on the inside. The best validation to a hard working man is the recognition of a woman.

And men want the approval of a woman just like women want the approval of a man. That's why she spends so much money on her hair, nails and makeup. She dresses her best so why shouldn't you?

The outside of a person is the best representation of how a person feels about themselves on the inside. It's easy to tell if a woman is lazy or if she's classy by the way that she treats her body and presents her external image.

What a man wears is part of his self expression. And you should be the type of man that enjoys looking good and smelling good especially if you want to attract a woman's attention.

You don't have to be in a suit or in your best clothes every day, but always look clean and be well kept. No one should ever look at you and guess what you represent.

People should look at you before hearing a word you speak and know what you represent. If you want to be treated as important and deserving of respect, then dress that way. If you want her to catch you, then you have to be catchable.

How can you stand out from all of the other men? Dress different! If you wear the same popular shoes that every man is wearing and wear your hair the same way every man is wearing it then how can she notice you?

You're Not Her Fan, You're Her Man

If she becomes the star of your life you'll compromise your manhood for her and she'll see you like a ho does a trick. The trick is willing to give up his power just for access to her pussy and that's why he's looked down upon.

Women want a man who won't compromise himself for anyone ever, even for her. When you compromise your masculine energy and give her feminine energy the leadership role then you've put yourself in a submissive position in her life.

The power of a man is his masculinity. And when you pedestalize her into the position of power you have made her the masculine energy of the relationship and you've become the trick.

A woman doesn't want to be your whole world because most women can't handle the pressure of being put on a high pedestal that she knows that she'll inevitably fall from. By nature women are insecure and have a low self esteem.

If you set too high of a standard for her self esteem you will create a pressure for her to be perfect that she can't live up to. She'll eventually rebel against the need to be perfect for you and leave for a man who doesn't worship her, but she worships.

She wants "you" to have the pressure of being perfect and not her. She wants the man to have all of the pressure to be perfect so he can be controlled by her guilting him with his mistakes, not hers.

If she has to be perfect all the time, she can't be freaky or make a mistake in the relationship because you'll guilt her for it as a form of control. Internally she knows that she's putting up a front of being a "good girl" just to win your favor.

But mentally she thinks the same nasty thoughts as men and she'll express them with the man who lets her be imperfect. This is why she likes bad boys because they show their imperfections up front. So she gets the chance to be her true self.

The only pedestal she wants to be on, is the pedestal over the other women in your life. She wants to be the number #1 woman in your life to increase her feelings of safety and security.

She wants to feel like you won't leave her because you prioritize her needs over the other important women in your life. Her whole ego and self esteem is tied into her feeling like she's irreplaceable in your life and you won't just abandon her.

But this plays into her ego. And by giving her the highest priority in your life she'll feel like she holds the cards to crumble you emotionally if she leaves you and the relationship.

It's a big mistake for a man to put a woman who's been in his life for a short amount of time over the women who's been in his life for a long amount of time. Especially if those women have shown up in your life's ups and downs.

Never betray your long term relationships like your family for a romantic relationship because it may not last. A family's love is forever, but the conditional love of a romantic relationship you'll have for a woman may not be.

That means to never elevate a woman over your mother, father, your sister, your brother, your grandmother, grandfather or any of your closest family members. This is too much power to ever give a woman who may be temporary in your life.

She wants you to be the star around other women so she can brag about what you do for her so they can be jealous. A woman naturally wants a man she can show off to other women, brag about and be proud of.

That's because women are very concerned about her friends opinions, and she wants them to look at her like she won you as a prize that they don't have. So the higher you are on the social scale the more important she feels having you next to her.

But if you are looking up to her, then her friends will look down on you because they know all her business. These friends know her truths and how she's struggled with her imperfections. They know that she isn't worthy of being made the prize.

They want a man who is strong that they have to chase his validation and his approval. Not a man who over compliments her and is always looking for her validation and approval of him.

<u>The Pimp Mindset</u>: She wants a man that she can respect. A man that she has to work to get his compliments, his time, his sex, his validation and his approval. A woman wants a man that she looks up to and can follow his leadership because he is on the pedestal.

A woman wants a leader she can follow and feel safe with. So if she has to take care of you and pay for your life expenses, supply the living environment, pay the bills and run everything in the relationship, she becomes the celebrity.

She's In Love With "Love" Not You

Women are not in love with the idea that most men think of "love" as. For men love is an action, and for women love is a feeling. This means that men and women not only love differently but see "love" in two very different and opposite ways.

A man sees love in a very tangible way as in what he does for her is a display of his love. But a woman sees love in a very intangible way as in how he makes her feel and how she feels about his love is "love" to her.

So a woman's love is based upon her own perceptions about what he does for her. Her love is internal and extremely easily influenced by her control and not his.

This is why so many men truly have no idea in their relationships how their women truly feel. A man thinks by him doing acts of love for her that it's going to be enough to keep her love, but it's not.

A man can give his woman everything that she wants and be an amazing guy who listens to her problems and shows up when she needs him to, but her love for him could still change because it's not based upon him.

It's based upon hormones in her brain. Women are in love with the internal "feelings" they call love that are in reality love hormones and not the actual actions of love as a man thinks.

These internal feelings in the brain are caused by at least 2 what are called "love" hormones. These love hormones she feels are named oxytocin and dopamine.

Sure you can do things to stimulate these hormones in her brain occasionally. But over time the same actions that stimulated them in the first place release less and less of these "love" hormones in her brain.

She felt this "love" high from the release of the love hormones with every new man she was in a relationship with, especially in the "honeymoon phase". This is why the honey moon phase was so easy.

Every time you did something for her the release of love hormones were at its peak. But over time her brain released less and less of these hormones especially as she got used to you and what you do for her.

This is why when the relationship goes bad she says I'm not in love with you anymore. All this simply means is that you don't make her feel the "love" hormone anymore.

You don't inspire dopamine releases in her brain to give her that "feeling" anymore when she sees you after missing your presence, like it did earlier in the relationship.

Ultimately the reality of the situation is that her "love" feelings for you have faded and you don't stimulate her brain anymore. You don't excite her anymore and she craves that "love feeling" again.

So she leaves you or goes out into the world to look for the man that makes her "feel love" again. And once she finds him she finds herself after some time not "feeling love" for the next guy anymore also.

So the cycle only continues after multiple failed relationships but she doesn't understand why. She doesn't understand why there's no "good men" in the world and believes that it's the men instead of her "love" chemical addiction.

She takes on the victim role and uses the men that she left in her path as the ones to blame for her lack of relationship success. But the truth is that she doesn't understand herself or her own female human biology.

She doesn't understand that what she feels is "love" never was the actual and factual describable actions of love. She was just in love with feelings, and not people.

That's why she could sleep with your best friend while you're together and say that you don't make her feel "happy" or "loved" anymore. She is chemically and hormonally driven by the brain as men and women all are.

But the difference is when it comes to "love", men and women are just wired differently. It wasn't always personal, it was just he made her feel the high and excitement of that "love" feeling again for a moment.

She can blame revenge or your lack of loving her for cheating, but in her search for a hormonal high the bigger picture and who she hurt wasn't her concern.

Her concern was to please herself with a new "love" high that was too hard for her will power to resist. This is why it's so important as a man to stay tapped into the energy and the actions of a woman.

You must always pay attention not to her facial expressions when you do something for her, but be paying attention to her energy when it happens. This is your master key to her true mindset.

Because when she changes what she thinks of you and how she feels about what you do for her, her love feelings leave soon after. Love for a woman is a feeling and not an action word.

Because her love is chemically and hormonally based upon her perception of you and what you do for her, a woman's feelings of "love" changes immediately when her mind changes.

And her changed feelings will always change the relationship. Her love is extremely fickle and based upon her internal judgement of you. If you move wrong in a way that turns her off on you and her together, her loves gone.

And there's nothing you can do to turn her love back on without her help. Her feelings of love for you and her together will change at the drop of a dime.

And any false move on your behalf, will change her feelings of love towards you altogether. And once a woman's feelings of "love" for you dissipate, she'll begin looking for the next man who makes her feel that "love" again.

This is why she can say confusing things like "I love you, but I'm not in love with you anymore." A lasting relationship can't be built upon "love" hormones alone.

Because then your relationship with her is built upon an easily changeable and quickly fleeting emotion. You have to build a strong relationship based upon facts and not feelings because feelings change, facts don't.

This means that you have to talk about what she specifically needs to feel loved so that she has to hold herself accountable to that standard. By making her define what actions equal love to her, she now loves with logic, not emotion.

She can't say later in the relationship that she doesn't "feel" love for you anymore based upon floating ideas in her head. She's made them specific actions you can do.

Now she can't use her "love feelings" as an excuse to leave a good relationship with a great man. Making her tell you what actions she needs to feel loved will force her to deal with the reality of love and not the illusion of love.

This means that if she says certain actions make her feel loved and if you do them, there's no way she can use excuses like she needs to find her happy, or she loves you but she's not in "love" with you as a reason to leave.

These are both excuses most women use to explain that she doesn't feel those love chemicals flowing through her strongly or at all anymore when she's around you.

These are all just learned and repeated excuses she's heard from other women. And because so many women use these same excuses to leave relationships with good men, they're now socially acceptable for her to use.

Now if she decides to leave the relationship with you she has to take full responsibility for not accepting your love actions and now she's the problem, not you.

If you did what she said makes her feel love, and it still wasn't enough for her, she has to redefine what actions equate to love in her life. That means that she's just a confused woman that doesn't know what she needs from a man.

She changed how she felt about what actions equate to love and that's her problem. Or she's just a cheater, deceiver and unsettled woman who can't pair bond due to her wandering eyes and desire for another man.

The better looking she is and the more pictures that she has of herself trying to look her best on the internet, the more "love" chemical options she has available to her.

This keeps her from having the ability to focus seriously on any one single long term relationship fully. She's an attention collector who preys on the desire of a mans attention to get her high of love chemicals.

She's become programmed from the social media algorithm to feel the emotional and physical highs of new likes and new attention. So it's extremely difficult for her not to cheat or to want to feel that "feeling" again.

It's like a drug user whose first high is amazing. But the issue is every single time that they do that drug after that it will never be as euphoric as the first time that high released the dopamine in their brain.

The drug user will need more and more of the drug over time just to be satisfied with the high. The same goes for good looking women, models and social media addicts.

The more highs she gets from likes, loves, dm's and male attention the more she needs. Because so many women are flooded with "love" chemicals constantly on social media they have become hardwired to be attention addicts.

They now pursue external validation more than a purpose or principle like class, sophistication or having wifely skills. Chasing the highs of likes, fame, and male sexual attention feels better to her than chasing relationships with good men.

This is why the amount of promiscuous women in this society has grown exponentially. Now showing your attractiveness to the public for attention and internet fame has became so much more frequent in this day and age.

So as a man don't confuse her intimacy, her sex or her confessions of love for you with her commitment. She can give you her body while another man has her mind.

That's because she's always loved the feelings of "love" and not you. She's in love with the high of "love". And like a drug abuser chasing the next high, she will chase the high of "love" over everything.

Because to her that high means her happiness. Now when you hear a woman say "I left you because I needed to find my happiness" or "I love you, but I'm not in love with you anymore" you'll understand what she really meant.

You don't get her high anymore and she had to find the next "love" high. And like a crackhead is always looking for their next high, she's looking for the male dopamine dealer that gives her the best and most pure high until she needs more.

Her Respect Weighs More Than Her Love

All love feelings fade over time naturally. But when she respects you she'll come back years later to see about you. That's because love feelings are replaceable but respect takes longer to fade.

Her respect can turn back to attraction, but her love alone cannot turn back into respect. Once a woman doesn't respect you, it's incredibly hard to make her desire to trust and respect you again.

You always want a woman to respect you more than she loves you. She is even much less likely to cheat on a man that she respects, versus a man that she only loves but doesn't respect.

When she stops respecting you as a man, she'll start exploring her options to find other men she looks up to and respects. This is why so many women leave relationships because they have lost respect for the men they're with.

Men get comfortable with their woman and then allow her to use the word love to manipulate them into doing things that lose her respect. All because they don't understand that if she doesn't respect you, she can't truly love you.

You must always keep her respect by standing up for yourself and your opinions during your conflicts with her. And never compromise your desires for her desires just to make her happy, because you'll lose her respect in the process.

When a woman feels like she loves you more than she respects you her emotions are in control, not her logic. You want her to love you deeper than her emotions. You want her to love you with her logic.

When she loves you with her logic, she'll love you with her mind and not just her body. That's because emotions are irrational and can change at any moment, logic doesn't.

This means that when it comes to her making decisions about the quality of the relationship, she'll base that decision on solid facts and not always changing feelings.

In this day and age the idea of love doesn't mean much. A woman can say that she loves you, but isn't in love with you. In reality all this means is that she cares for you, but doesn't respect the man that you are.

This means that she doesn't really love you because she doesn't know what love truly is. Logical love is understanding, patient and unconditional. But emotional love is fickle, selfish and based upon feelings not facts.

Most women base the idea of love on emotions, feelings and specific actions. You won't change the way a woman loves, so add her respect with her love so she loves you with her emotions and her logic.

This way you capture her whole mind, not just a small part of it. A woman who respects you even if she leaves won't make it a difficult process. Her respect for you will have her checking on you later in life when you're not together.

But a woman who doesn't respect you will do things like sleep with other men in your bed, talk to other men while you're together and do things to hurt you on purpose.

A woman's respect for you weighs much more than her love for you. As a man, always remember that a woman's love is emotional, situational and conditional, but her respect is logical, solid and intentional.

Your respect taps into her logical mind and it will stay there forever as long as you don't do things to be disrespectful to her. Always be a logical man when dealing with her. Never allow her to get you into your emotional self.

Seduce Her Mind And Her Body Follows

Women use their bodies to get what they want from men, while men have to rely on their minds to get what they want from women. So it's your job to use your mind to get what you need from her.

It's why a nerd can get a beautiful woman. He listened to her and she felt comfortable and vulnerable enough to open up her legs to him. You have to give her the inner attention that she craves instead of the outer attention most men give her.

This is especially true if she's beautiful. Just complimenting her alone won't work because a pretty woman knows that she's beautiful and even a cute woman knows that she's only cute.

So by telling her that she's more beautiful than what she thinks she is she knows you're using the game of flattery to get in her panties. Play the reverse game by being the man who doesn't over compliment her looks and her body.

Be the man interested in what's in her head. Be the man that's looking to understand who she is on the inside and you'll automatically gain access to her body as a result. Most men never tap into her interests, only her body that's why they lose her.

If you possess her mind by listening to her weaknesses, her traumas, her past and her interests the body comes for free after that. Most guys are only looking at her body and ignore her mind, but they miss the gold mine.

The mind controls the body. So when you gain access to the mind of a woman you gain free access to her body, her desires and her emotions. Now you can tap into her mind at any time to bind her to you.

Men are physical by nature and women are emotional by nature. So a woman needs emotional stimulation before being sexually stimulated in most cases.

So act as if you're interested in her mind more than her body and you'll get access to the key that opens the doorways of her body. Her mind is more valuable than her body. And by showing more interest in her mind she'll give you her body.

Find Out:

-What's her personality?

-What does she value in life?

-What are her desires?

-What are her fantasies?

-What are her dreams in life?

Technique: Let her talk as you listen for facts about her and then remember key topics she brings up. All people, but especially women love when you get them talking about themselves. Listening to her gives you an edge on her thought life.

Watch her body language when she brings up certain topics she's passionate about and look at things in her environment that help you get an idea of what her interests are.

Is there tattoos, earrings, shoes, pictures, favorite colors, etc and use them as conversation topics to get her talking . You do this so you can get her to trust you.

It's less about exactly what she says and more about her feeling comfortable opening up to you. A woman who opens up her mind to you deeply will open up her legs to you in no time. Just be patient and consistent indoor listening behaviors.

<u>The Pimp Mindset</u>: This is playing the reverse game on a woman. By acting as if the pussy isn't the only goal, she will inevitably begin to trust you with her body. Most men approach wanting the body and never stimulate the mind out of greed.

Be patient and wait it out strategically. If you listen to her, she'll see you as the "different" kind of guy until she falls in love. But really you let her fall in love with herself and her ability to be around a man she can talk about herself with. That's Real Game!

Exactly How To Seduce Her Mind

Step #1: Build a connection with her mentally before sexually. Because it's hard for a woman to disconnect from a man mentally. But it's much easier for her to disconnect sexually because of promiscuity culture.

Your job as a man is to give her the best experience she could ever have mentally and physically with any man. This helps you capture her mind and thoughts regardless if she's with you in the future or not.

Step #2: Build a connection with her sexually through love making. Love making is different than normal sex because making love connects to her mind, her body and her soul. Lovemaking is on a different dimension when you understand what it truly is.

Sexually it combines the words you say to her during sex, the way you hold and take control of her body during sex and making sure she orgasms. When you make a woman orgasm her body bonds chemically to you.

Use this chemical bond to your advantage by making her climax every time you both have sex.

This means that you have to worry less about you orgasming and more about her climax.

A man has a much easier time climaxing because of the way a man's dick is stimulated. Because a woman's pleasure zones to climax are inside of her body and it's often on you to find the spots that bring her to a climax.

By letting her sit on top of you and ride is a great way to do this. If you let her use your dick to stimulate her own pleasure zones, she can take the charge she needs to find what angles get her closer to a climax.

The female orgasm is extremely elusive to even her. Some women don't even climax during sex and she won't likely have an orgasm just from a man's dick alone.

Use her body as a tool to learn what she desires and make sure that she reaches an orgasm every time during sex and her body is yours. Because her body will crave you!

<u>Step #3</u>: Have deep conversation where you let her talk and reveal all of her secrets to you. By being open and listening to her you'll become a safe place for her thoughts, her beliefs and more importantly her desires.

Once you understand her wants and desires you've entered her inner life. Let her reveal to you the woman most people will never get to see. You can't seem like you're judging her. Be her non judgement zone and she'll tell you all of her secrets.

Possess her mind and you will automatically take hold of her body. Her mind is her main computer and holds all of her hidden secrets that she keeps away from the outside world.

Learn her thoughts and her desires and you'll know everything about her. A person can only speak what they think in their minds so just listen and let her tell you.

Step #4: Bring something new to her life. This makes her look at you like a hero that's trustworthy and reliable. This means teach her new information, a new outlook on life, a new hobby or take her on a new experience.

When you teach her something new she gains a respect for you that translates into mental and physical attraction. Now when she tells others about what you've taught her, or goes to the places you showed her, she'll think of you.

Women want a man who can teach and lead her to new thinking and new experiences. Not a man who she has to be the teacher and leader of because that's boring to her.

When a woman has to teach a man she sees him as her son, instead of a man she wants to have sex with. If she learns new things from you it makes her feel like your daughter and you her father.

All women crave the teachings and protections of their father especially if she never had a father present in her life consistently and desired to have one.

Her attraction to you will fade if you don't teach her anything new because she has to appreciate your mind to value it. Your mind is what sets you apart as a man from more attractive and wealthier men than you.

She has to respect your opinions and your beliefs on everything she does. This means that she has to respect your mind and your thoughts enough to want to listen to your thoughts and ideas.

If she doesn't want to listen to you willingly, then she sees you as weak and beneath her. This means that you don't have a hold of her mind and over time you will lose your connection to her body.

Capture her mind and automatically her body follows. If you take your time to know who she really is in her mind, you'll have the power to control the relationship.

Listen And Learn Her Desires

A woman's desires are what lead her life choices, behaviors and attitude in life. Women who desire material things can be rewarded with these things she desires to keep her attention.

But remember that material things only give her temporary highs. Women who desire less material things have more emotional desires. Rewarding her emotional desires for her good behaviors are an easy way to keep her attention.

Fulfilling a woman's emotional desires last longer than rewarding her material desires. That's because a woman's happiness by nature is built upon emotional pleasure.

Pay attention to what kind of woman she is. Is she emotionally motivated or is she materially motivated? Does she desire physical touch, talk and walks or new purses, random gifts and surprise dinner and dates?

Even if she likes material things it's emotionally driven at its core because it makes her feel wanted and desired by the man she's with. But listen to her and look at her lifestyle.

What emotion are her desires driven by? The desire for more material things, emotional things or is she driven by the simple things in life like physical touch or words of affirmation?

Understanding her basic desires is your magic key to turn her emotions on whenever you need to encourage, entice or motivate her to keep doing whatever you want her to keep doing. Her desires show you what to reward her with.

Knowing her basic desires also tells you if she desires something you don't have or don't have much of like time or money. If you don't have enough money she'll leave you for a man with more money.

If you don't have enough time for her, then she'll find a man who does have the time for her. Your awareness of her desires helps you understand what she believes will make her happy even for the moment.

That means if the things she desires are pulling strong enough on her emotionally away from you, she'll fill those desires even if it means hurting you in the process.

For example if she has a strong enough desire for negative obsessions like sex, money or drugs you will always lose her to those desires in the long run guaranteed.

If her desires are to obtain money, fame, status, looks and the validation of others you will lose her to those desires also. Her desires will always pull and tug on her mind until they're fulfilled.

This is why any man who gives a woman everything he can give her but what she truly desires, loses her to the man who fulfills her desires of what she truly needs.

The reason why so many good men get cheated on is because the woman he's with, desires a good man mentally and emotionally but a bad guy sexually and he has no idea because he's not paying enough attention to what she desires.

Your only job is to learn and know her desires from the beginning. Understanding her motivations and desires helps you stay ahead of her in the game when her desires present themselves around you both.

And when you need her to feel motivated, appreciated and rewarded, by understanding her desires you have an advantage over most men in relationships.

Most men don't know how to motivate their woman with her desires when she needs it. They never take the time to focus on anything but their own selfish desires for sex.

So ultimately they lose their women to other men who can fulfill her mental and or emotional desires because they saw it as important to get to know their woman as deeply as possible for their own advantage.

Trigger her desires for your own advantage by rewarding her with her desires. This is all social media has done with the reward and consequence cycle.

They reward women with their emotional desires of acceptance, validation and approval. Because of their understanding of a woman's desires, social media platforms are now billion dollar companies.

Use the same winning formula that they use by liking what she does right and not rewarding behaviors you don't like. Motivate her by rewarding her good behaviors with the desires of her heart.

Reward her for her great work, loyalty and for proper behaviors just like women do men with leveraging sex. We all need to feel rewarded anytime we're doing something consistently or we'll lose our motivation to act.

She needs a reward so she has a clear reason in her mind why she's with you. It's your job to make her staying with you rewarding. The key is to only reward her for good behavior.

Don't ever just randomly reward her with something that she didn't earn. If you just reward her randomly your rewards will lose its value and its strength over time.

Only reward her for doing something that you asked her to do, and any other actions that you want to keep encouraging your woman to do. When you do this she starts to see and feel that giving to you is rewarding her life in some way.

This is called positive reinforcement. You're rewarding a good behavior to motivate the person to keep doing it. This is actively using the reward response in a persons brain to keep them wanting to do things for you.

If you don't motivate and reward a woman with her desires to stay with you, then another man will reward her with her desires to leave you. Women need something to work for in the relationship to stay focused and engaged on you.

Lead Her With Words, Not Money

She will expect you to keep up the ways you try to impress her. So from the beginning set up a standard you can live with. Never set up an unreal standard because it always comes back to hurt you when you can't keep it up.

This means that whatever you lead with, is what a woman is going to respect and expect because a woman is always measuring your worth and your purpose in her life.

So if you show her that your worth in her life is money and your purpose is to share it with her through gifts and expensive dinners, she'll see you as a trick.

A trick always leads with his wallet because he's willing to give up his value just to have sex with her. So inevitably the trick loses because he gets played for his money and his gifts until it's over.

In reality she only fell in love with his money and gifts, not him, his game or his personality. She never learned to respect him as a man because she was blinded by the money and gifts.

So the gifts and the money is what she respected because that's what he showed her was his value and his contribution to her life. A woman never respects the trick, just like a ho never respects the trick.

This means if you lead a woman with your wallet then she'll never respect you, or your words because she'll respect your wallet. This is what you taught her by leading with your money and wallet instead of your words.

Even when you talk she won't really desire to listen unless money or gifts come along with your words in some way because there's no incentive for her to listen to you.

So she's not submitting to you, she's submitting to the money and that's it! Once the money and gifts are gone, why would she stay? If what she benefits from isn't available anymore what's going to keep her around? Nothing!

By leading with your wallet and spending your money in exchange for time with her you'll never get your moneys worth for it. You'll only end up being used and feeling resentful because she never developed respect for you.

But it's not her fault because you tried to win her approval with money. Your words must always lead the way and not your wallet if you want her to respect you for who you are. You're not a trick who pays what he weighs.

You're a pimp and you can never pay anyone to stay, especially a woman who'll take your money and still not respect you for sharing it with her. Your game is what leads the way and because you're the value she has to pay you to play.

A woman who listens to your words and believes in you is the worthy woman to keep around. That's because your words are more likely to last a lifetime than your money.

Money comes and goes, but it's the game that comes for free out of your mouth that she must desire to follow. If she follows your wallet she'll only stay until the moneys gone, but if she follows your game she may stay forever.

Real Game Separates You From The Lames

The game of women and getting women is no different from the mating rituals in mother nature. As a peacock struts his feathers to impress the female peacock, a man has to show his worthiness to earn the woman's attention.

You are no different, but there are certain techniques in this game that give you an advantage and help you stand out from the crowd. That has to be the goal for you on this journey into the game.

You have to understand that men are 99% the same, but it's the 1% that get their choice of all the women. That's because these men talk, walk, think and have the aura of a man who's different.

A different and real man is something males all over the world try to imitate but they can hardly duplicate. A real man is a real man regardless of who needs help, what business he conducts or who he is trying to seduce.

A real man and not an imitation is unapologetically him so he needs not lie ever, especially to a woman who he should never fear. A real man is consistent and steady.

He's not about using the game for any way other than to advance himself, his family, his community and his life experiences. Because the game is rewarding and learning the game itself will reward a man's life greatly if he dedicates himself to it.

Spend your time wisely on activities that further your levels of manhood instead of going backwards like the other 99%. If you do this with some consistency, the game will make sure that you'll have everything you need.

How To Give Her Game

Step #1: Be you always with no mask. If you're not down with the real you, she won't be either. When a woman meets a man that believes in being his authentic self, regardless of who likes it, she admires his courage.

Your courage signifies honesty and authenticity to her which she sees as strong, bold, powerful and attractive. This is what masculinity feels like. Too many men are locked up in a mental "nice guy" prison.

In nice guy prison a man doesn't feel like he can say and feel how he wants without fearing consequences from his woman or the people around him.

These "nice guys" find themselves with repressed emotions and depression, because they feel like they can't be who they really are and still be accepted.

A real mans game comes from his ability to be free from the constraints of this nice guy prison that keeps the average man scared and weak when dealing with his life and with women.

When he embraces that he doesn't have to be perfect or nice all the time because he needs everyone to accept him he automatically gets pushed into his true masculine power.

Step #2: Don't hesitate to act on a choosing signal. Jump on the action immediately when she chooses up on you. If you jump on an opportunity when it's hot you avoid any distractions between your game and her, like anxiety.

If she's ready to play the game with you, play it win or lose. Most men wait and sit back waiting for her to approach, and that's fine if you're out being cool to attract a woman. But, if the woman shows interest initially in you, take your shot.

It's all a game of hit or miss. Just like in basketball, you miss every shot you never took in the game. As long as you have something slick or comical to say you'll have plenty of women waiting on you to give them more game.

Step #3: Talk that shit to her. You have to be able to flirt and flow through emotions and logic at the same time. The issue with most men is they are either too logical or too emotional without allowing themselves to flow through all emotions.

Just because a man is expected to be logical doesn't mean that he is always running on logic. Women run off of emotion first then logic, so if you can't flow with both she'll get bored with you quickly.

She craves your ability to rebalance yourself and your emotions easily because she has a hard time doing the same. Flirt, talk serious, talk sexual, be mean. Give it all to her and she'll love your genuine ability to be yourself and not one dimensional.

If you ever wondered why bad guys do girls wrong and they come back over and over it's because he can talk shit to her the way that she likes. He can give her the ups and downs that create relationship excitement that fills her daily need for variety.

She wants both love and war, not just love and peace like most men think is so important. Now the difference between the bad guy and you is you'll know what you're doing because you're learning the game.

Step #4: Lead her with the thoughts that feed her. Never force her to do what you ask because that's not using game. If you're using game you are planting seeds in her mind all the time.

You do that by telling her your future plans and things you want to buy or plan to do so she can start executing for you. But you must always do it strategically.

<u>The Pimp Mindset</u>: Real game sees the woman's mind and body like a garden and you are the gardener. If you plant the right seeds and cut the weeds by giving her direction with proper motivation, she will in return give you dedication.

By nature a woman is a people pleaser and she wants to please you so you approve of her. And she will do anything to please you if she thinks making you happy is buying you what you want. But you have to plant the seeds in her mind of what you want.

Step #5: Feed her mind with motivation to gain her dedication. Feed her motivation and inspiration through rewards by gifting her the little thing she likes to keep her focused on accomplishing the goals you set for her.

This will keep her mind fueled with goals to accomplish and incentives to do so. When your game is effective it offers her a way out of her old ways of thinking and being and into the happiness you provide instead. This is done with rewards.

Step #6: Sell her the dream of a better life if she works with you and not against you. When you meet a woman you should already have things for her to do as a part of your life. Put her to work on your dream, but sell it as both of your dream!

You can't be the kind of guy sitting around being happy just because you got a girlfriend, but you have no direction to lead her. Immediately let her know the blueprint during conversations so she can help you accomplish your goals faster.

Have ways that she can help accomplish these goals with specific tasks she can execute for you. In this way you test her ability to be a team player. If she's not a team player you'll know quickly to let her go so you can protect yourself from a lazy woman.

Lying Isn't Real Game, It's Lame

Too many weak men acting like they're real men has watered down the idea of what's real. Now the fake looks more real than the real looks real. And the fake have tried to make the real look corny or boring.

Part of this is due to the modern media and the extremely effective marketing strategies of the entertainment industry because it's built upon marketing an illusion or real.

But they've sold the illusion with shiny things so well, that people believe in the lies more than they believe in the truth. So to set yourself apart from most men, the world and other people you have to become the truth.

Don't try to manipulate anyone using lies because it only works short term. Eventually most people will figure out they're being lied to. So stop lying to get a woman, she'll never stay!

Give her 2 choices:

1. Accept the truth and stay

2. Reject the truth and leave

Regardless of what she chooses you have to be okay with her leaving. As a man, stand up for the truth even if that means losing people who love the lies because you're always better off.

Most of the time she will accept the truth and stay because they've never been treated this way. Refuse to play the lying game, it's for losers. Lying to someone is the easiest way to lose their respect and their admiration.

If you stand firm on your principles of truth, you don't have to ever worry about getting caught up in the lies and rumor tricks people use to try and destroy your character.

A woman will always respect you if they know they'll always get the real from you. That's because they've already dealt with the men who look like the real but are really fake. So if you show yourself as real and you stay the real you'll keep her trust.

Why The Lying Game Doesn't Work

Too many other men have tried to use this same lying game just to get in her panties. They already sold her the same dreams of who he is and what he can offer her. So you can't do the same thing if you want to be looked at as different than them.

Be real with who you are and what you are always, there's never any exception. You shouldn't have to lie if the game is truly in you. You have to use your common sense and ask yourself "Why would I use the same game that comes to mind immediately?"

What comes to your mind immediately is the same game that every other man used that failed before you. Because if she had a man that had real game she wouldn't be out looking for a new man in the first place.

Your first thought is every mans first thought. Even if you get her with lies in the beginning, it's only a matter of time before your lying game looks lame to her. Because if you're a liar it will eventually show.

What's in the dark will always come into the light to be revealed! All lies have an expiration date, while the truth always arrives right on time. Even if she doesn't catch your words, your behaviors will show your lies eventually.

That's because you'll do the same things that every other man running the lying game does. Once she sees the switch in your behaviors she'll become a detective determined to find the truth.

Her intuition will eventually notice different behaviors patterns that the past lying men displayed. You may get away with fake words, but you can't hide body language.

For Game To Work It Has To Be:

1. Clear - The destination that you want to take a woman and the goals of your game must always be crystal clear to you and her

2. Condensed - Your game can be explained in a few words effectively, and it can be stated quickly

3. Continuous - Your game has to be ongoing continuously so it can be installed, programmed and adjusted for any situation and any person

Simps Lack Real Game

Simps lose the respect of their women and get treated poorly because they relied on the external and material symbols of legitimacy to gain access to pussy, instead of focusing on truly becoming what a woman will value long term.

Legitimacy Establishes: Who you are and what you have to offer the dating marketplace. Every person has to offer the dating game some sort of legitimacy that you can offer to others as evidence that you're real and not just using fake game.

What do you present to others that establishes your legitimacy in the dating game? Is your game based upon fake symbols like money, material possessions or your looks? Or real game symbols like your swag, your energy, your personality?

Symbols of Real Game:

- Style
- Your body
- Status (reputation)
- How you carry yourself

Symbols of Fake Game:

- Cars
- Clothes
- Houses
- Vacations

Alone these are symbols of fake game, not real legitimacy because they can be bought. Real game can be taught and not bought. If you can only buy a woman things but you can't teach her anything, she'll only use you for your money.

You can use fake game to attract a woman but if you never developed the necessary skills to keep a woman's attention she'll eventually go missing.

That's because she respected your symbols of the game, but never your real game.

Money comes and goes but your game helps to keep the flow of the relationship alive. You can have the most money, the nicest cars and the best looks, but if you lack a personality you'll lose her every time because she'll get bored.

So many simps think that if I look good, have the most money and drive the nicest car I can get women, but they don't understand the game at a deeper level. Getting a woman's attention is much easier than keeping a woman's attention.

Simps don't see the importance of having real symbols of legitimacy like character, personality, masculinity, purpose and authentic confidence to attract women. This makes them only one sided and one dimensional when dealing with women.

They only understand the easiest part of the game which is to look the part, but they don't have the other side of the game which is to act and truly become the part. And once a woman sees that he's an actor and not the real thing she feels fooled.

The Pimp Mindset: Use both sides of the game so a woman feels like being with you is a rare opportunity that she needs to take advantage of.

You do this by having real legit game based off of your personality and not only fakery.

What material possessions you have is built to attract her attention, but if it's all you have she'll use you for it. But if you have the items of real legitimate game then she'll see you as a man that she needs to keep around because of your value.

Learn How To Play "Hide The Dick"

Thinking pussy first gives her pussy power over you. It's always purse first, ass last. This means that you have to stop trying to give dick to every woman and focus on how she can add to your pockets instead.

If you're stuck in dick thinking then your actions, words and mindset will be full of I want some pussy intentions. She can feel this energy easily because every man comes with the same horny dog energy.

The Pimp Mindset: Show her the opposite energy to make her see you as different. You can make her want your dick in time by leading with your big head instead and using strategy and self restraint.

Most men act like horny dogs wagging dick in her face even if it's in your mind. She can always tell when your dick is out mentally because you'll talk like it.

Your dick has a time and a place and not every place is the time to lead with your little head. Being pussy minded fogs your judgement and can put you in the position of a trick to be manipulated by an intelligent woman.

This can lead to making big mistakes with women, some can be deadly. Don't be so motivated to get pussy that you get blinded to the facts in your face like most men. You can't think like most men if you want to think and move like a pimp.

Dick thinking ruins men everyday because they look past her flaws to get the draws. Control your dick thinking so you can take her pussy power away. Her pussy is the only game she really has to rely on to keep a mans attention.

She believes her pussy is more powerful than your dick because most men act like it. Sex is an even exchange of energy not a one sided event. She's been taught her pussy has more power than your dick, show her the facts.

When you show her that you value your penis more than you value her pussy she'll have to reconsider how much she wants her pussy over your dick.

She has a pussy already so it doesn't benefit her unless it meets your dick, understand that clearly! Switch the game up on her and place more value on your dick than her pussy.

Now she'll pursue your dick because she has no more power or pussy leverage over you.

Remember you're switching the game up on her and using her own manipulative sex game on her.

She uses sex and the fantasy of getting sex from her to get money, clothes, time and energy from a man all the time. She doesn't know what to do when she meets a man who treats her like a trick.

Every man in her past has given her sex when she wants it. So she's used to being in control of when and where she gets sex but now you're in control. Don't give her sex whenever she wants it.

Make her wait and show you why she deserves to get dick from you. Now you're the ho and she's now the trick. You've switched up the game on her brain!

Make Her Invest Her Time & Money In You

The more time and money she spends on you, the more attached she will be in the long run. That's because she's made a time, an emotional investment in you.

The more time, emotions and money that a woman invests in you, the less likely she'll leave that investment quickly. This is the opposite of how most men play the game.

Normally a man does all of the investing in her then he gets attached, while she isn't. He spends all of his time and money trying to wine and dine her to show her that he's worth her time.

But inevitably all he's doing is showing her that she's the valuable one in the relationship. Because a valuable person isn't trying to convince the other person of their value.

They know their value and require others to invest in them. You're the valuable one and if you want her to see you that way then you let her invest in you first.

Let her spend her money on you, let her do the most of the phone calling and let her make the most effort to find time to spend with you. Let her invest in you, not the other way around like most men think they should do.

<u>The Pimp Mindset</u>: If you let her do the majority of the investing then she'll be hesitant to take a loss on her investment in you. Let her do the work to earn her role in your life, not the other way around.

Let her make time to spend with you so that her time investment is high. A woman will value her time invested in you more than her financial investment in you.

So make her put in as much time investment as possible. She'll be hesitant to give up quickly on you because she doesn't want to invest that much time and money in you and get nothing for it.

If you don't keep her investment in you high she will intentionally do just enough to get you attached to her then ease up. This is how she gets you and so many other men attached in the beginning thinking that she's wifey.

All she did was let you make all of the time, money and emotional investments into her. She just played the good girl role to keep you investing in her until you were hooked.

Then later once you both got serious in the relationship she switched up her actions and her attitude on you. This is why you let her do all of the investing in you because she will always put in a lot of effort to win your approval at first.

Because in most cases a woman will always put her best foot forward on the gas pedal when she meets you because her feelings are involved. She's in the submissive role of needing your approval so she's willing to do the bulk of the effort.

But once she's gotten comfortable and her logic kicks in then she'll ease up on the gas pedal to see if you'll give back. So selfishly when she invests in you, she's looking to get back at least the time she spent on you and financially.

This is why you make her invest her time and do 80% of the effort in everything. This sets the standard for the relationship because she sees that you're the valuable one to be invested in, not just her like she's used to with most men.

Make her earn your pleasure and your company instead of you trying to earn hers. If you do this when dealing with a woman you'll get both. A man has to use the same game a woman uses on her to win.

If you use her own game against her then she won't see it coming from a mile away. Women aren't used to men dealing with her using strategy. Because most men are dealing with her with lust and desire.

Let her invest her time and money in you and you'll always reap the rewards of it. Remember that value doesn't market itself because it's valuable and not everyone can afford it.

Make her invest in your value and she'll value you, your time and your energy because she had to work for it. If she doesn't want to do the investing in you, let her go for one who will.

You Don't Own Her, You Just Loan Her

Loyalty is very, very rare so don't put all of your trust in her today, because you never know what tomorrow will bring. Always remember that a woman is likely to go to another man eventually once her feelings fade away.

Don't ever let her in too close to ruin you and never tell her all of your personal business. Always keep in mind that if she leaves you, your most intimate personal business and your outside reputation is always going to leave with her.

Especially if she's looking to ruin you she'll know how to because you let her in too close. Now she knows exactly what your weaknesses and your vulnerabilities are. When she splits, she's going to tell her next man and everyone else your business.

Always let her tell you all of her business, instead of you telling her all of your business. Keep your big secrets and vulnerabilities to yourself by never telling her what your weaknesses are, your biggest regrets or the wrongs that you've done in your life.

Always stay a stand up man in your life and in her eyes. It's your job to make sure that you don't do things that you'd be ashamed of her telling others that you've done. Protect your reputation and never tell her about the people you've done wrong.

Stand tall and stay true to your morals and values to keep from giving her access to negative things that she can say about you to ruin the way people look up to you. And always stay prepared for her betrayal just in case it happens or doesn't.

Absolute and unwavering trust is a commodity that you can't ever afford with a woman. Always expect and prepare for a woman to leave you just in case so your life isn't disrupted. This is playing the game like a pimp instead of a simp.

You and your life can't afford unexpected betrayal, so always be prepared for it by expecting it just in case. And don't expect her loyalty if you're abusive to her. If you're playing her too hard and rough she'll run off when she gets the chance.

Abusing a woman in any way gives her all the ammunition she needs to ruin your chances with other women, because they all talk to each other about the men they've dealt with. Your name will come up and she'll always make herself the victim.

There's No Loyalty In This Game

Loyalty is very, very rare so never put all of your trust in one woman because you never know what tomorrow will bring. Always remember that a woman is likely to go to another man eventually regardless of how strong your game is.

That's because curiosity always kills the cat! Her curiosity of other men will pull her towards disloyalty at all times. And one day she might let her mind and her imagination about another man get the best of her.

Don't be fooled by her vows of loyalty to you because it's game! And because a woman can leave at any moment, never tell her all of your personal business.

Because when she leaves you and the relationship, your personal business, your secrets and your reputation is always going to leave right along with her.

And one thing that you can surely count on with a woman is that she'll talk about your business to the next man she's with. She'll tell them all the good, the bad and the ugly of your life if you tell her too much because you trusted her too much.

Let a woman tell you all of her business, instead of you telling her all of your business. And then make sure that you keep any of your problems, worries, weakness and your game plan to yourself regardless of how down she has been.

So always stay prepared for her betrayal in this game just in case. Trust is truly a commodity that you can't afford because it's more expensive than you can imagine.

3 PIMP PICK UP TECHNIQUES

"Never walk up to a woman, present yourself to a woman."

-Pimp Rosebud

Courting Technique: **How To Get A Woman Obsessed**

This is the hot & cold technique built to get a woman emotionally attached to you and then you back off. What getting her into you and then backing off creates is an attachment to you. And it gives to the dominant power in the relationship.

This will give her the feelings of rejection which most women have a difficult time dealing with. Rejection makes her ego chase you harder to find out why you rejected her.

And sometimes it makes her want to get even with you by showing you she can get you. So you have both of those factors in your favor when you use this technique.

This only works only if you have:

1. Style/swag

2. Personality

3. Charisma

4. High Value

5. Self-esteem

6. Confidence

The Play: Do all the pursuing in the beginning then evaluate her level of interest in the first 2-3 weeks.

Ask yourself is it high or low based upon how hard she pursues you back.

How much is she calling you and how much time is she trying to spend with you. If it's a lot then you got her! Once her interest is high, then back off your pursuit of her.

When you back off to a comfortable level for you, observe her interest level again. How hard is she pursuing you since you backed off? The harder she pursues you, the more interested she is in you.

But don't back off too soon. If she isn't showing a high level of interest in you yet then you have to give it more time for her to commit. Backing off too soon won't give her enough time to get mentally attached to the idea of you two together.

Backing away from her has to be like a dimmer switch and not like an on/off switch. You have to be sure to slowly back away so it's gradual as she gets more intense in her feelings for you.

In the beginning you're doing 100% and she's doing 20%. But as her interest and her pursuit raises, you must lower yours to 30% and stay at the level that you're comfortable keeping her at.

This will make her chase your validation because she'll notice that you're not as available as you used to be. She'll start thinking that it's her fault you're backing off so she'll work harder to get your attention.

The Formula:

Step #1: Draw in

Step #2: Draw back after her attachment

Step #3: Allow her to draw in towards you

Step #4: Set your comfort level of giving

As long as you don't give her enough of your time to satisfy her time wants from you, she'll stay focused on winning your approval to get more of your time and more of your energy.

<u>The Game</u>: Her feelings of rejection automatically put her in the position of submission and give you the power. That's because you're creating an emotional attachment in her.

This technique gives her mind enough time to start imagining you two together as a fantasy. Now she wants to try and make the fantasy in her mind come true.

So when you back off from her, she will pursue you harder because now she's already built an image in her mind of you two together. She's imagined what sex with you will feel like and she's imagined what life with you will be like.

Women build a life together with a man in her mind first because they are mental and emotional people. If you give her enough time to imagine you two together enough times she'll have a much harder time letting the fantasy go.

Club/Bar Pickup Technique: **The "Fly Fishing" Strategy**

In this strategy you're required to have a high level of confidence and swagger. You need the confidence to look straight at the woman you want badly with a high level of confidence and self esteem.

You need the swagger in your game to reel her in. This comes with dressing the part and having a calm and cool demeanor. You'll lure her in by showing choosing signals so she'll approach you because she knows that you're interested.

Step #1: Sit at the bar facing the crowd and spot the girl that you want

Step #2: Get her attention with eye contact. Then after she notices you noticing her…….

Step #3: Raise your eyebrow, smile and then turn your back and return to your drink, phone conversation, etc. Don't wait for her to smile back, just slowly and smoothly turn around and look away from her and the crowd.

If she's interested in you back then she will respond to you with her approach. Women are very forward when they want a man that's already shown interest in them.

That's because it lowers her chances of being rejected when she knows a man likes her. A woman always wants to feel wanted first before she approaches a man.

Step #4: When she approaches you, be ultra laid back and comfortable because the game is on!

In conversation:

a. Be able to flow with her. Stay slow and methodical in your conversation and make sure that you keep eye contact and use it effectively. Use humor, flattery and slick smiles during the conversation.

b. Listen to what her body language is saying, not just her words. Observe and ask yourself how much is she interested in me? As long as you keep her attention you got her. She already saw something that she liked in you so just close the deal.

c. Take control of the conversation. Ask her questions about her and don't spend the whole time talking about you. Show her that you're into her. If she asks you questions answer them and get back to her immediately. And make sure to use your eyes provocatively.

You have to stay smooth the whole way. If you get nervous just take small deep breaths. And remember that it's all a game, you win some and you lose some. If she takes the hook you got one, if not just repeat the process with another girl.

Conversation Tip: Wink at her if she's into the conversation and watch her melt. Body language helps to get her focus more on what you're doing instead of only on what you're saying. This helps to draw her in to you fully.

Manipulation Technique: **Reversing The Game On A Gold Digger**

Also Known As:

- Clout chasers
- Gold diggers
- Social Climbers
- Black Widows
- Jezebels
- Man eaters

She thinks that she will get your:

- Power or importance
- Connections

- Resources
- Fame
- Money
- Time

She thinks that she will get some of what you have, just because she's in proximity to do so. And she's hoping to take what you have because these women are social climbers that use their bodies to manipulate men out of what they want.

<u>The Game</u>: Let her play herself by thinking that she's playing you. But the fact is that you're playing her the whole time. You're acting like a

possum who's playing dead, but is only playing that way to manipulate the predator chasing it.

#1. Figure out which of the few items on the list she wants from you

#2. Once you know what she wants from you, feed her little doses of it with dreams of more in the future as you get what you want

With these women the game is to never give her fully what she thinks she's using you for once you know what it is exactly that she wants. You're the drug dealer and she's a drug addict that you keep dependent by feeding her controlled little hits to keep her high.

While you're feeding her what she wants, make sure you establish a pattern of behaviors in her through repetition. You can do this by never giving her what she wants without getting what you want from her first.

Example: Give her gifts or money only after sex. When you get sex give her something the next day that she's using you for. Never give her a high if she does not give you what you want ever.

Her Manipulation Technique: She'll ask for more out of you but what she really means is that she wants more of what she's trying to use you for. The small hits aren't as effective as before, so she needs an increase in drugs.

She has to use emotions to manipulate you because this is her only tool at this point and it works on 99% of men. Express that if she wants more from you, then she has to show you more and do more for it.

Once she stops wanting to earn her rewards she'll leave or ask for more. Then let her leave because her game was only based on getting superficial things out of you. She was just using you anyway.

Why Women Do This: These women get adrenaline hits when they beat men out of his possessions and energy. No different from how a man feels when he wins a competition. This is only her playing the game of men at the highest level.

She's not playing the game like the low level women who give up their bodies for nothing or no benefit to themselves. She's no better but she feels like she is because she gets money for her body, but it's still the same lost woman inside.

THANK YOU FOR READING

If You Received Useful Tools In This Information, Please Give Me A 4-5 Star Rating!

★★★★★

This serves as a reward for an author. It takes hours and months, sometimes years of no pay to put together books for the purpose of sharing information you see as important to the world.

Please just take out a minute of your time and please leave a quick positive review. If you didn't receive any value from this book then dm me on instagram @theprofessorofpimpology to tell me why.

Either way, Thank you tremendously for taking out the time to read this information and knowledge. If you really took this information seriously and you applied the key principles into your daily life, I KNOW you are seeing results.

So again, I thank you for your interest in learning and any investment in applied knowledge will always be a winning investment.

NOTES